HOW TO DRAW

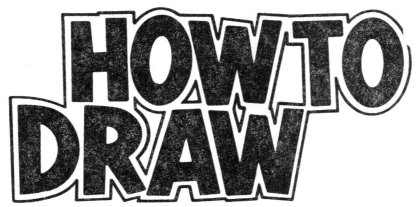

Not everyone is an artist. . .but almost anyone can learn to draw by following step-by-step instructions. If you can draw a fairly good circle freehand (you can practice first!), you can draw the characters in this book. And with lots of experience, who knows? You may become an artist after all.

You will need a good drawing surface. Use strong paper with a slightly rough surface (like the paper in this book). Pencils slip on a surface which is shiny; erasers make holes in paper that is too thin.

Pencils with medium-soft lead work the best (e.g. No. 2). Have a pencil sharpener handy to keep points sharp. A ruler will help you draw straight lines. Be sure to have a good eraser. Add a good light source and you're ready to begin.

Circles, ovals and pears are shapes used most often in drawing. Lines for neck, arms and legs form a simple skeleton to hold the shapes together. Always start drawings by *lightly* sketching the basic shapes.

Now let's get started. You can work right in this book on the spaces provided on each page. There are extra blank pages in the back of the book for more practice. Have fun!

TO DRAW MICKEY, BEGIN WITH SIMPLE SHAPES.

ADD DETAILS.

MICKEY IS A MOUSE OF MANY MOODS.

ARMS TAPER TO TOP
OF SHOULDERS

LEGS TAPER
TO HIPS

MICKEY'S HANDS
ARE LARGE,

JUST THREE
FINGERS AND
A THUMB.

SHOES ARE FLAT
ON THE GROUND.

MICKEY IS A
MOUSE OF
ACTION.

WHEN SEATED,
FEET DO NOT
TOUCH THE FLOOR.

MICKEY WEARS MANY HATS.

FIT THEM
BETWEEN
HIS EARS.

DRESS MICKEY IN MANY OUTFITS.

MINNIE IS DRAWN LIKE MICKEY.

SHE HAS LONG
EYELASHES,
BUT NO
EYEBROWS.

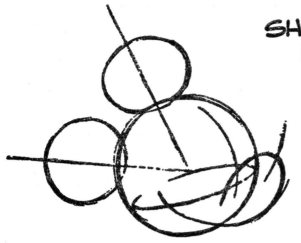

SHE WEARS
A HAIR BOW.

SHE IS 3 HEADS TALL.

HER SKIRT DRAPES OVER
HER TAIL, AND SHE
WEARS HIGH-HEELED
SHOES.

1.

2.

3.

1.

2.

3.

MORTY AND FERDIE ARE FUN TO DRAW.

NEPHEWS ARE 2½ HEADS HIGH.

1.

2.

½

1.

2.

½

MORTY AND FERDIE JUST REACH MICKEY'S SHOULDER.

TO DRAW DONALD, BEGIN WITH SIMPLE SHAPES.

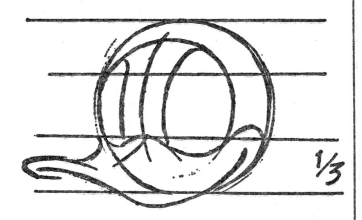

1/3

DONALD'S BILL IS ABOUT 1/3 OF HIS HEAD.

TUFTS OF FEATHERS ON FRONT AND SIDES

DONALD'S EYES
HELP SHOW HOW
HE FEELS.

DONALD IS NOT QUITE
4 HEADS TALL.

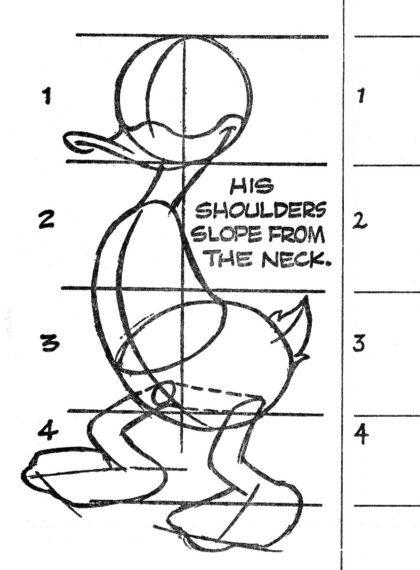

HIS
SHOULDERS
SLOPE FROM
THE NECK.

1

2

3

4

1

2

3

4

HIS LEGS ARE JOINED TO
THE SIDE OF HIS BODY.

ONALD WEARS
SAILOR CAP
AND MIDDY.

HIS
HANDS ARE
LONG AND
SLENDER.

JUST
THREE
FINGERS
AND A
THUMB

ACTION POSES
TO DRAW...

MORE ACTION POSES

DAISY IS DRAWN LIKE
DONALD.

DAISY HAS EYELASHES.
FEATHERS CURL AT
THE SIDE OF HER HEAD.

SHE WEARS A HAIR
RIBBON.

DAISY 'EARS HIGH-HEELED SHOES.

1

2

3

4

1.

2

3.

4.

HER FEATHERS ARE RUFFLY.

HUEY, DEWEY AND
LOUIE ARE FUN
TO DRAW.

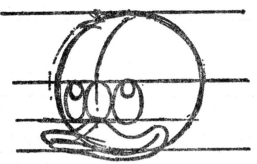

EYES ARE SPACED ONE
"EYE" APART AND ARE
IN THE LOWER HALF
OF THE HEAD.

NEPHEWS ARE 2½
HEADS TALL. LEGS
ARE SHORT; KNEES
LOW.

1

2

½

1.

2.

½

WHEN STANDING,
THE NEPHEWS
COME UP TO
DONALD'S BILL.

DAISY AND DONALD ARE ALL
DRESSED UP.

DAISY IS NOT AS
TALL AS DONALD.

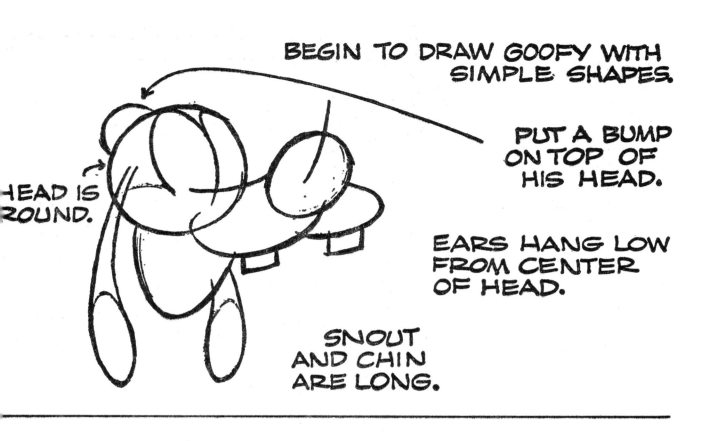

BEGIN TO DRAW GOOFY WITH
SIMPLE SHAPES.

PUT A BUMP
ON TOP OF
HIS HEAD.

HEAD IS
ROUND.

EARS HANG LOW
FROM CENTER
OF HEAD.

SNOUT
AND CHIN
ARE LONG.

EYE-BROWS ARE RAISED.

THREE LONG HAIRS STICK OUT ON FOREHEAD.

EYELIDS DROOP

PUPILS ARE CLOSE TOGETHER.

THREE HAIRS ON HIS SNOUT

TWO SMALL HAIRS ON EARS

GOOFY IS 9 HEADS TALL.

NECK IS LONG AND THIN.

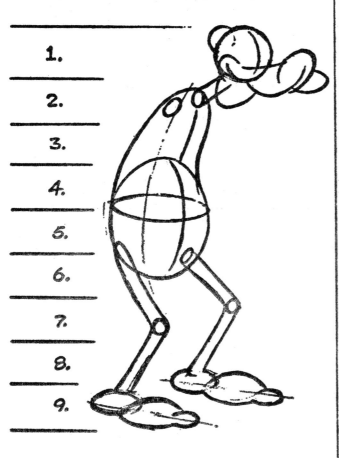

1. _____
2. _____
3. _____
4. _____
5. _____
6. _____
7. _____
8. _____
9. _____

THE
MIDDLE
OF HIS
ROUND
TUMMY
IS
HALF-
WAY
MARK.

1. _____
2. _____
3. _____
4. _____
5 _____
6 _____
7 _____
8. _____
9. _____

GOOFY SLOUCHES
FORWARD A BIT.

CLOTHES
HANG ON HIS
BODY.

HAT
IS
ONE
HEAD
HIGH.

HANDS
LARGE
AND
GLOVED.

JUST THREE
FINGERS AND
THUMB

LONG,
FUNNY
SHOES

GOOFY
EXPRESSIONS

HERE IS PLUTO.

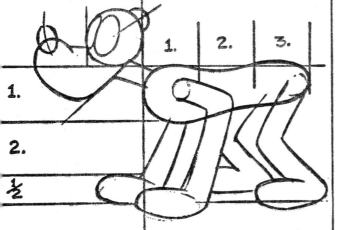

	1.	2.	3.
1.			
2.			
½			

	1.	2.	3.
1			
2.			
½			

NOTICE HIS
HEAD BUMP
AND EARS.

DON'T
FORGET
HIS
TAIL.

THE CHARACTERS ARE DIFFERENT
HEIGHTS WHEN SHOWN TOGETHER.

PRACTICE PAGES